Step by Step

Pasta

Step by Step

Pasta

Janet Marsh Lillie

Bloomsbury Books
London

Page 2: Bolognaise Sauce with Saffron Fettucine(p. 17). One of the classic Italian pasta sauces to accompany any pasta.The preparation for this delicious dish is shown on the endpapers.

This edition published in 1994 by
Bloomsbury Books
an imprint of
The Godfrey Cave Group
42 Bloomsbury Street, London. WC1B 3QJ
under license from
Harlaxton Publishing Limited

Harlaxton Publishing Limited
2 Avenue Road, Grantham, Lincolnshire, NG31 6TA
United Kingdom
A Member of the Weldon International Group of Companies

First Published in 1994

Publisher: Robin Burgess
Project Coordinator: Barbara Beckett
Designer: Rachel Rush
Editor: Alison Leach
Illustrator: Maggie Renvoize
Jacket photographer: Rodney Weidland
Inside photography: Jack Sarafian
Food stylist: Janet Marsh Lillie
Produced by Barbara Beckett Publishing
Colour Separation: G.A. Graphics, Stamford, UK
Printer: Imago, Singapore

British Library Cataloguing-in-Publication data.
A catalogue record for this book is available from the British Library

Title: Step by Step, PASTA
ISBN: 1 85471 318 3

Step by Step

Contents

Cook's Notes

Measurements

All spoon and cup measures are level. Standard spoon and cup measures are used in all the recipes. I recommend using a graduated nest of measuring cups: 1 cup, ½ cup, ⅓ cup and ¼ cup. The graduated nest of spoons comprises 1 tablespoon, 1 teaspoon, ½ teaspoon and ¼ teaspoon. For liquids, use a standard litre or imperial pint measuring jug, which also shows cup measures. As the metric and imperial (US) equivalents given are not exact, follow only one system of measurements within the recipe.

Ovens should be preheated to the specified temperature. The heat on top of the cooker (stove) should be set at medium unless otherwise stated.

Ingredients

Pasta cooking relies on simple ingredients. If you are making homemade pasta, you will need good quality, plain (all-purpose) flour and eggs.If you buy dried durum wheat pasta or fresh pasta from the supermarket or specialist delicatessen, make sure you get a variety of long, flat and short shapes (see page 9). Your pantry should contain the following ingredients: cans of peeled tomatoes for convenience—and emergencies; tomato paste, virgin olive oil, red and white vinegar, balsamic vinegar; cans of sardines, anchovies and tuna in oil; jars of capers, black olives and pimento stuffed olives; rock salt; peppercorns; nutmeg; pine nuts and almonds. Fresh vegetables, in particular firm, ripe, round or plum-type tomatoes are essential.

You will also need good quality minced (ground) beef, veal and pork; poultry and fish; cheeses like Parmesan, pecorino, ricotta; single (light) and double (heavy) creams; chicken or beef stocks made with stock cubes or powders; a selection of sausages like mortadella and salami; Parma ham (prosciutto) and bacon (pancetta). Herbs, in particular basil, oregano and rosemary are used fresh; if fresh are unavailable use half the stated quantity of dried herbs. Use freshly ground black pepper whenever pepper is listed; add salt and pepper to suit your individual taste; use fresh chillies if possible. If you substitute dried chilli flakes or powder for fresh chillies, halve the quantity.

Chicken Niçoise with Lasagne (p. 45). Lasagne makes a unique pasta base for this tomato-wine chicken casserole.

Introduction

Everyone enjoys pasta. It is one of the simplest of dishes to prepare and takes little time to cook in boiling water. Pasta is economical and easy to store; being high in energy and low in calories (kilojoules) it is nutritionally good for you, comes in over 600 different shapes and types and what's more, it's absolutely delicious.

The instructions are clearly set out. There are step-by-step guides to different ways of presenting pasta. Many of the recipes are photographed at the preparation stage to show a special technique as well as the finished stage to show what the dish looks like and how to present it for the table. There are handy hints about how to peel, seed and cut different ingredients and useful information such as how to judge when your pasta is cooked, and the different types of pasta that you can substitute for those given.

A glossary of terms is on (p. 47) for you to look up any term that is unfamiliar. There is a list of recipes (p. 5) for your reference. Be sure to read the information on measurements and ingredients before you begin cooking.

The origins of pasta are not really known, although records show that it was eaten in Roman times. Some believe that Marco Polo brought the art of pasta-making back from China when he returned to Italy in the thirteenth century. Few believe this theory. Historians say that an ancient tool, seen in the frescoes of an Etruscan tomb, is a macaroni maker. If so, this would indicate that pasta in its simplest form had an established place on menus in Imperial Rome.

Modern machinery now produces a wide variety of pastas from different basic ingredients.

Pasta secca is dried pasta made commercially from the endosperm of the durum wheat kernel. This is ground into semolina flour and mixed with water to make the dough.

Pasta all'uovo is egg pasta, made from flour and eggs. You can either make it yourself at home, or purchase it ready–packaged, fresh or dried, from supermarkets, specialist shops or delicatessens.

Wholewheat pasta is usually factory–produced as packaged dry spaghetti or lasagne sheets.

Flavoured pasta is either semolina or egg-based. The flavour comes from natural vegetables like spinach, from tomato purée, pumpkin, or even dried red pepper (capsicum, bell pepper). Saffron is added to give colour and variety.

The word 'pasta' simply means 'paste'. It is one of the great culinary miracles that a simple paste of flour and water, or flour, eggs and oil, can be transformed into a dough and rolled out and formed into so many shapes and sizes. You will find threadlike vermicelli, broad sheets of lasagne, thick tubular ribbed rigatoni, golden ribbons of fettuccine, and a host of fancy shapes such as ditalini, tiny quadrucci, farfalle and many more. There are also the well-known stuffed pastas, like ravioli and tortellini.

Different sorts of pasta are interchangeable so if you can't buy the one stated in the recipe you can substitute whichever is easily obtained or appeals to you, bearing in mind the relative size

Spinach Lasagne (p. 46), which can be prepared ahead and heated when required, makes an enjoyable meal with salad and a light red wine.

and shape of the pasta used in the recipe. You can, for example, use penne instead of rigatoni and linguini instead of vermicelli.

The following list includes all the varieties used in this book.

Long Pastas
Bucantini: Large thick hollow spaghetti which goes well with oil and garlic-based sauces.
Capellini: Fine ribbon pasta. Capelli d'angelo means angel's hair, which is the thinnest variety.
Fettuccine: Flat ribbon noodles. It can also be sold coiled in 'nest' shapes. It is ideal with tomato, seafood and cream-based sauces.
Linguine: Very thin, narrow ribbon noodles eaten with delicately flavoured sauces.

Different Shapes of Pasta

Dried pasta: farfalle, top, and ruoti/trulli.

Dried pasta: conchiglie, top, and ditalini.

Dried pasta: spaghetti, top, and tagliatelli.

Fresh and stuffed pasta: ravioli, top, and tortellini.

Spaghetti: The most common variety of pasta, it comes in various thicknesses. It gets its name from the Italian word 'spago' meaning string.

Spaghettini: Known also as fedelini, it is finer than spaghetti, and goes well with fresh tomato and basil sauces.

Tagliatelle: The most common form of flat ribbon noodle, slightly wider than fettuccine. Tagliatelli verdi (green) has puréed spinach added to the basic dough. It is also available in narrower widths when it is called tagliarini.

Vermicelli: Very similar to spaghetti in length, but finer in width. Vermicelli means 'little worms'.

Short Pastas

Conchiglie: The word means 'shells'. It is a concave short-ribbed pasta, used with all kinds of sauces including tomato, meat and seafood.

Ditalini: Means 'finger of a glove' or 'thimble'. Ditalini are small, stubby, hollow tubes, commonly used in soups.

Eliche: Means 'propellers'. These are spiral-shaped and go well with most tomato or cheese-based sauces.

Fusilli: Hollow spaghetti shaped like a spring. They go well with sauces containing light garlic and oil, tomato or seafood.

Farfalle: Bow or butterfly shaped pasta. Farfallini are smaller. They go very well with fresh tomato or cream sauces.

Macaroni: Also known as maccheroni, it is a wider, hollow version of spaghetti. It can be cut into short or 'elbow' shapes of varying lengths. It goes well with tomato and meat sauces and can be used in baked pasta dishes.

Penne: Short, plain or ribbed, tubular pasta with the ends cut off diagonally like a quill. They are similar to rigatoni. Pennette are a small version.

Quadrucci: The odd shapes and bits left over from pasta making. They are often chopped into squares and used in soups. They are also available dried.

Rigatoni: Derived from the Italian word 'riga' meaning lined, they have a ribbed surface, are

slightly larger than macaroni (maccheroni) and are ideal with chunky vegetable and meat sauces.
Ruoti/Trulli: Shaped like wheels they complement oil, garlic and light cream or vegetable sauces because of their ribbed and intricate pattern. Ruotini is a smaller version used in soups.
Spirale: Pasta lengths twisted together to form a spiral. They are ideal with tomato sauce.

Filled Pasta

Ravioli: Well-known pasta dumplings, they are usually square and can be stuffed with almost anything. The most popular filling is ricotta cheese and Parmesan or spinach.
Tortellini: Shaped like little hats, these contain a variety of fillings such as chopped chicken breast, pork or mortadella, and seasonings.
Both ravioli and tortellini are cooked in boiling water and served with butter and Parmesan cheese or a variety of sauces.

Baked Pasta

Cannelloni: Means 'big pipes' and is the largest of the tubular pastas. It is widely used for stuffing and baking all varieties of sauces. They are also available dried and ready to fill.
Lasagne: Often homemade but usually available dried or fresh in supermarkets. It is the broadest of the ribbon pasta and sold in flat sheets either plain, ridged or with crimped edges. It comes in various sizes, or as one continuous sheet which is cut to the size of the dish. This pasta is used for baking in layers with different sauces and cheese or rolled around stuffings for baked cannelloni. Lasagne verdi (green lasagne) is also common.
Lasagnette: A smaller version of lasagne, it is a flat ribbon pasta with a ruffled edge.

When you cook pasta, you need certain basic pieces of equipment. Most of these you will already have in your kitchen.
Saucepans: a large saucepan for cooking pasta in. The basic proportions are 4 litres/7 pints/ 4½ quarts of water to every 500 g/18 oz of pasta; two or more medium-sized, single-handled, heavy–bottomed saucepans with lids.
Cooking cutlery: a long-handled fork to stir the pasta as it cooks; a perforated or slotted spoon to scoop out and drain portions of pastas like lasagne and tortellini; two sharp knives for preparing ingredients for sauces; several wooden spoons for mixing and stirring sauces.
Other equipment: a large colander (perforated strainer) with handles and legs, that will stand by itself in the sink—a stainless-steel one is preferable; a cheese grater; a fine sieve (strainer) or food processor for pureeing some sauces.
  When you are making fresh pasta you will need: a large pastry board, table top or other steady surface; a long wooden rolling pin; a pastry wheel for cutting pasta to give it wavy edges; a good knife with a broad blade for cutting pasta evenly and steadily.
  Before you learn the simple rules for successful pasta cooking, you should also experiment with the sauces. There are no real hard and fast rules. You can mix and match any pasta with prepared sauces from available ingredients. Pasta is fun to cook and everyone can enjoy doing it.

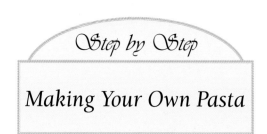

Step by Step

Making Your Own Pasta

There is nothing quite as delicious as homemade pasta. Making it is a challenge at first but don't be discouraged. With practice you will succeed. The following recipe uses the traditional method, but you can simplify the process by using a food processor or blender. Use the ingredients below and follow the technique given on (p. 13).

Making Pasta

500 g/18 oz/4½ cups plain (all-purpose) flour
2 teaspoons salt
5-6 very fresh eggs, lightly beaten

2 tablespoons olive oil
Rice flour for rolling out pasta

Combine the flour and salt on a work surface. Shape into a mountain and push your fist into the centre to make a hollow. Put the eggs and oil into the hollow.

Using your hands or a fork and a circular motion mix in the eggs gently, gradually bringing in some of the flour as you go. Start from the centre and work outwards. Use one hand for mixing and the other to hold the flour in place and prevent the eggs from escaping.

When the egg mixture has thickened, start folding the mass together by lifting up extra flour with your hands and pushing it into the mixture. When all the flour is mixed in, form the dough into a ball. Using both hands, push down with the heel of your palm and begin to pull and knead the dough. Keep turning, kneading and folding until the dough is very smooth and soft and springs back when touched. This will take a good 8-10 minutes.

Rest the dough under a cloth for 5 minutes. This makes it easier to roll out later. Divide the dough into two or three portions and roll them out separately.

Cover your hands, the work surface and rolling pin with rice flour. Flatten the ball of dough with your hands. Begin to roll out, always rolling away from you. Turn the dough slightly to the right after each roll so that it begins to form a circle. Continue rolling until you have a perfect circle. Fold it in half and roll out again. Continue until the dough is 3 mm/⅛ inch thick or as thin as possible.

Roll the dough up on itself very carefully like a Swiss roll (jelly roll). Cut to the desired width with a sharp knife—tagliatelle 12 mm/½ inch; fettuccine 6 mm/¼ inch; linguine about 3mm/ ⅛ inch and tagliarini a little thinner.

Place the pasta on to a clean dry tea-towel (dish cloth) or plate. Leave to dry for 20 minutes to prevent the pasta sticking during cooking. Cook as required (p. 14).
This quantity of flour makes about 750 g/1¾ lb pasta.

Making your own pasta. Always shape the flour into a mountain, then push your fist into the centre to make a hollow for the eggs and oil.

Food Processor Method

Place all the ingredients in the food processor or blender. Process until mixture resembles breadcrumbs. Tip out onto a floured board. Press the mixture together in your hands to combine into a dough. Divide the dough into three sections and knead each as described (see page 00) for about 8 minutes until the dough is soft and springs back when touched. Here you can either roll it out by hand (p. 12) or use a machine.

If using a machine, press or roll the dough out to 6 mm/¼ inch thickness. Place in a pasta rolling and cutting machine following the machine instructions until the dough is rolled out into a long thin piece. Cut into strands as narrow or as wide as you like. Lay these on a clean dry tea-towel (dish cloth) or plate. Leave to dry for 20 minutes and cook when required (p. 14). *Makes about 750 g/1¾ lb.*

Making Fresh Pasta

Shape flour into a mountain, make a hollow and add eggs and oil.	*Gently mix the eggs and work in the flour.*	*Knead dough by pushing it with the heel of your palm. Keep turning and kneading.*	*Roll out the dough until it is 3 mm/⅛ inch thick.*
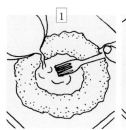	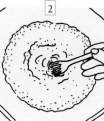		

Bring the water to the boil with the lid on. *Put in pasta and a few drops of oil. Boil rapidly without lid.* *Drain the pasta through a colander (perforated strainer).* *Transfer to a warm serving bowl or individual bowls.*

Cooking Pasta

Following two simple rules when cooking either fresh or dried pasta will give you perfect results every time. First, use plenty of liquid. Pasta must swim in its cooking liquid. Allow 125 g/4 oz pasta per person. For 4 people you will need to use a lidded pan that will hold 500 g/18 oz pasta in 4 litres/7 pints/4½ quarts water. If you like, add 4 teaspoons of salt and 4 teaspoons of oil to the water. Cover and bring to the boil.

When the liquid is boiling vigorously throw in all the pasta at once (unless you are cooking stuffed pastas, lasagne or cannelloni). This ensures that the pasta cooks evenly. Stir well to prevent the pasta from sticking, cover and bring to the boil again quickly over high heat. Remove the lid, and start timing the cooking, stirring pasta occasionally. Don't leave it to cook itself. Pasta needs your constant attention.

Second, remember that timing is all-important. It is impossible to give exact cooking times. These depend on the size, shape and type of pasta. Dried pasta for example can vary from one manufacturer to another so always check the packet instructions. Fresh pasta on the other hand takes about half the cooking time of dried.

There is, however, an easy test to tell whether your pasta is cooked. Pull out one piece of pasta and bite it. If it is tender, but still firm, with no hard, white uncooked central core and if it is slightly resistant then it is *al dente*, which simply means firm to the bite. Not everyone enjoys their pasta *al dente* but when overcooked it is a disappointment to eat.

When it is cooked, drain your pasta immediately into a large sieve or colander (perforated strainer), shake gently to release all the moisture, transfer quickly to your warm serving bowl or platter, pour sauce over it and serve.

Storing Grated Cheese. *Cheeses such as the hard-grating Parmesans and pecorinos, when purchased in a piece, can be finely grated and frozen in small amounts in sealed polythene bags.*

Classic Sauces

There are four classic sauces that are served with pasta. Many variations on these classics have evolved in kitchens throughout the regions of Italy over many, many years. You too, can learn their secrets. Make a double quantity of these sauces in advance and store them in sealed containers in either the refrigerator or freezer for use at a moment's notice.

Pesto Genovese with Ruoti

Traditionally, sardo, a Sardinian cheese made from sheep's milk, was used with Parmesan to give this sauce a pungent flavour. Using Parmesan only produces a milder-flavoured sauce.

About 20 basil leaves
1 garlic clove
30 g/1 oz/¼ cup pine nuts
30 g/1 oz/¼ cup grated Parmesan cheese

3 tablespoons olive oil
400 g/14 oz Ruoti or any pasta
Parmesan cheese, to serve
Basil, to garnish

Process the basil, garlic, pine nuts and Parmesan cheese in a food processor or blender until finely chopped. With the motor running, add the olive oil in a stream until ingredients form a thick purée of pesto. Cook the pasta until *al dente* (p. 14). Just before draining, add 3 tablespoons pasta cooking water to the pesto and stir until combined. Drain the pasta and transfer to a warm bowl. Toss with the pesto and garnish with basil. Serve with more Parmesan cheese. *Serves 4.*

To cook pasta successfully, use a large saucepan with a lid and plenty of water—4 litres/7 pints water per 400 g/14 oz pasta.

A selection of the classic Italian cooking sauces, including Béchamel (below) and Fresh Tomato Sauce (p. 18).

Béchamel Sauce

Known as bescamella in Italy, this sauce is ideal for baked pasta dishes such as lasagne and cannelloni.

60 g/2 oz/¼ cup butter
60 g/2 oz/½ cup plain (all-purpose) flour
500 ml/17 fl oz/2¼ cups milk

1 small onion, studded with 5 cloves
Salt and pepper
Generous pinch of nutmeg

Melt the butter in a saucepan, blend in the flour to make a smooth roux or paste, stirring continuously. Cook over a low heat for 1 minute. Remove and leave to cool. Pour milk into a clean saucepan and add the clove-studded onion. Heat until bubbles appear around the edge of the saucepan. Remove from the heat and strain the infused milk into a bowl. Whisk the milk into the roux all at once, return the pan to a low heat and stir continuously until the sauce thickens and boils, about 10 minutes. Season with salt, pepper and nutmeg.
Makes about 500 ml/17 fl oz/2¼ cups sauce.

Bolognese Sauce with Saffron Fettuccine

*Originating in Bologna this classic sauce or 'ragu' is perhaps one of the best known in the world.
Everyone has their own favourite version of it. Some are strongly tomato-based and others, with the addition of
a tablespoonful or two of cream and nutmeg, have a more subtle flavour. Sliced mushrooms add further interest and
give a different texture. You can serve this 'ragu' with any type of spaghetti.*

1 tablespoon olive oil	4 ripe tomatoes, peeled and chopped (p. 30)
1 onion, chopped	2 tablespoons chopped parsley
1 garlic clove, crushed	½ teaspoon basil or oregano
1 carrot, diced	250 ml/8 fl oz/1 cup stock
1 celery stick, diced	125 g/4 oz/1½ cups button mushrooms, sliced
450 g/1 lb/4 cups minced (ground) beef, or veal and pork	Salt and pepper
	400 g/14 oz saffron fettuccine
125 ml/4 fl oz/½ cup milk	Parmesan cheese, to serve

Heat the oil in a saucepan, cook the onion, garlic, carrot and celery for 5 minutes or until onion softens. Add the meat and stir continuously until it changes colour and browns lightly. Add the milk and cook until it has almost evaporated. Put in the tomatoes, parsley, basil and stock and stir until the sauce boils. Cover and simmer for 15 minutes. Add the mushrooms and cook for a further 15 minutes. Season with salt and pepper. Cook the fettuccine until *al dente* (p. 47). Drain and transfer to a large warmed platter or individual serving bowls. Spoon the sauce over the pasta. Serve the Parmesan cheese separately.

Serves 4

Variation

Stir 1-2 tablespoonfuls single (light) cream and about ¼ teaspoon nutmeg into the sauce.

Making Béchamel Sauce

Melt butter, blend in flour and stir continuously for 1 minute.	*Remove from heat and cool. Heat milk and onion in separate saucepan.*	*Whisk the milk into the roux and return to low heat.*	*Stir continuously until sauce thickens. Season.*

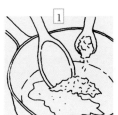  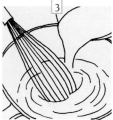 

Fresh Tomato Sauce

Italian cooking relies on tomatoes, particularly in the southern regions. You can prepare this basic salsa pommarola ahead of time and refrigerate. Use this light tasty sauce within a week of making it.

750 g/1¾ lb fresh ripe tomatoes
1 large carrot, chopped
1 large onion, chopped
2 celery sticks, chopped

30 g/1 oz/½ cup Italian (flat-leaf) parsley
Salt and pepper
4 tablespoons olive oil

Put the tomatoes, carrot, onion, celery and parsley in a saucepan. Bring to the boil, cover and simmer for 40-45 minutes. Remove from the heat, press through a sieve (strainer) and discard all the seeds and vegetables. If not using the sauce immediately, place it in an airtight container and refrigerate until needed. Just before using the sauce, season with salt and pepper and add the oil. Pour the sauce on to the pasta.
Makes about 750 ml/1¼ pints/3 cups.

Quick Tomato Sauce

When fresh, ripe tomatoes are not available or when time is against you, an acceptable alternative can be made by using canned peeled tomatoes and concentrated tomato paste.

2 tablespoons olive oil
2 onions, finely chopped
3 garlic cloves, crushed
2 bay leaves
1 teaspoon basil leaves

1 teaspoon salt
1 teaspoon sugar
4 tablespoons tomato paste
2, 400 g/14 oz cans peeled tomatoes, cut into pieces
125 ml/4 fl oz/½ cup dry white wine

Heat the oil in a saucepan. Cook the onion and garlic for 5 minutes or until the onion softens. Add the remaining ingredients, bring to the boil, stirring continuously. Simmer the sauce, uncovered, for 20 minutes. Remove the bay leaves. Use the sauce as needed.
Makes about750 ml/1¼ pints/3 cups.

To Seed Tomatoes (Concasse). *Peel tomatoes (p. 30) and cut them in half. Squeeze the tomato gently to make the seeds come out, or scoop them out with a teaspoon. Flatten each half gently and cut into small cubes. Use as required.*

Pasta in Soups

There is an old Calabrian song about the glories of soup. Translated it says , 'Soup does seven things: it appeases your hunger, satisfies your thirst, fills your stomach, cleans your teeth, makes you sleep, helps you digest and puts colour in your cheeks.' It is small wonder that soup is regarded as such an important course in Italian cuisine. Pasta in a soup gives a feeling of warmth and well-being. Some pasta soups, known as minestra, are almost meals in themselves. Minestrone, which means 'big soup', is a typical example. It can be simple or complex depending on what ingredients you put in, and whether you add pastina such as penne, farfalle or macaroni to give extra body. Other soups, known as brodo, are light, clear broths. They rely for their flavour and interest on good stock and the addition of any of a variety of tiny pastina shapes such as ditalini, ruotini, farfallini or quadrucci.

Pastina in Broth

Add tiny pasta shapes known as pastina to give nourishment and flavour to a light and appetizing soup. Always start with a well-balanced stock the better the stock, the better the result. The amount of pastina simmered in the stock can vary, depending on taste. As alternatives to pastina, try fresh, dried or homemade tortellini.

1 litre/1¾ pints/4¼ cups good beef or
    chicken stock

200 g/7 oz any shaped pastina
60 g/2 oz/½ cup Parmesan cheese, finely grated

Bring the stock to the boil in a large saucepan. When it is boiling hard, add the pastina by pouring it from about 15 cm/6 inches above the saucepan, stirring continuously. Boil for about 10 minutes or until the pastina is very soft. Ladle the soup immediately into individual bowls and serve the Parmesan cheese separately.
Serves 4.

To Purée a Tomato Sauce. *Strain cooked tomatoes into a colander (perforated strainer) over a bowl. Ladle or spoon them into a food processor or blender. Turn the 'pulsing' switch or alternatively switch the machine on and off every second or two until the contents are blended to the desired consistency. This is determined by the amount of liquid you have added to it during the process. Alternatively, the cooked ingredients may be pushed through a sieve (strainer) to achieve a soft uniform mass.*

Pea and Bacon Country Soup

This soup is a light minestra in which tiny square-shaped pasta known as quadrucci are cooked. If you have made your own pasta, keep the left over bits and cut them into tiny squares to add to this simmering soup. The squares may not be as even as the bought product but they will give this soup a truly homemade look.

30 g/1 oz/2 tablespoons (or ¼ stick) butter
125 g/4 oz belly pork or thick rashers (slices)
   bacon, rinds removed, chopped
1 large onion, chopped
1 celery stick, chopped

1 sprig fresh parsley, chopped
1 litre/1¾ pints/4¼ cups beef or chicken stock
500 g/18 oz peas, shelled
500 g/18 oz quadrucci
Parmesan cheese, to serve

Melt the butter in a large saucepan. Add the pork or bacon, onion, celery and parsley. Cook gently until well browned, then add the stock and peas. Stir continuously until boiling. Simmer for about 10 minutes. When the peas are tender, add the pasta. Cook for 5-6 minutes or, if using homemade pasta, about 3 minutes. Serve immediately with the Parmesan cheese.
Serves 6.

Onion Vermicelli Minestrone

Tiny button-sized onions are best for this warming soup. If you can't find these in the shops, buy pickling onions instead. Break the vermicelli or capellini, the finest ribbon pasta, into short pieces before adding to the soup. Spaghettini, spaghetti or linguine are other alternatives you can use.

400 g/14 oz baby onions or pickling onions,
   peeled
1 litre/1¾ pints/4¼ cups water
125 ml/4 fl oz/½ cup olive oil
125 ml/4 fl oz/½ cup Fresh Tomato Sauce, (p. 18)

Salt and pepper
200 g/7 oz vermicelli
60 g/2 oz/½ cup Parmesan cheese, grated

Place the onions in a large saucepan and add the water, oil and the tomato sauce. Season with salt and pepper. Cover and allow to cook over a low heat until the onions are almost completely tender, about 30 minutes. Break the vermicelli into short pieces, add to the onion mixture and stir together thoroughly. Season with a little more salt and pepper if necessary and add more water if the vermicelli seems dry and likely to stick. When the vermicelli is almost cooked, remove from the heat and leave to stand for a few minutes. Sprinkle with the Parmesan cheese and serve at once.
Serves 4.

Pea and Bacon Country Soup. An easy minestra using a pasta called quadrucci.

Chopping Onions

Peel the onion under a running tap leaving the root intact.

Cut the onion in half vertically and lay flat on chopping board.

Slice onion vertically, not cutting the root.

Slice onion horizontally to make dice.

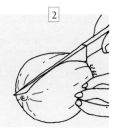

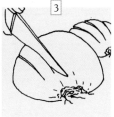

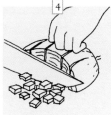

Pasta Salads

Since pasta has become so well-known and popular there is no end to the ways it can be used. Pasta adds interest to salads. Its shapes and colours complement shiny red tomatoes, glossy green and yellow peppers (capsicum, bell peppers), dark green broccoli, crisp spinach or lettuces. Add colour, strong flavour and interesting texture to *al dente* pasta with light creams, the finest of oils, flavourful vinegars and tangy lemon juice. Your salads will become gourmet dishes. Salads can be prepared in advance. Cook the pasta and rinse in cold water to prevent it cooking further in its own heat. Leave it in a bowl of cold water till you need it. Rinse it thoroughly before adding the other salad ingredients and the dressing. Serve these salads the way the Italians do—with plenty of crusty bread and a bottle of crisp chilled white wine or a light red wine.

Fusilli Salad with Sun-Dried Tomatoes and Rosemary

The pasta in this salad is also known as corkscrew pasta because of its shape. Remember to toss in the oil and balsamic vinegar dressing just prior to serving, otherwise it will discolour the courgettes.

500 g/18 oz fusilli
4-6 courgettes (baby marrows, zucchini), sliced
1-2 garlic cloves, finely chopped
2 teaspoons rosemary leaves, finely chopped
3 tablespoons virgin olive oil

10-15 sun-dried tomatoes, cut into strips
Pepper
3 teaspoons balsamic vinegar
Mixed lettuce leaves, to garnish

Cook the fusilli (p. 14) for about 6 minutes. Add the courgettes and cook for a further 6–8 minutes until the pasta is *al dente* and the courgettes are just tender but still crisp. Drain the fusilli and courgettes, rinse in cold water and allow to cool. Mix the garlic, rosemary, oil, sun-dried tomatoes, pepper and vinegar together in a bowl. When ready to serve add the fusilli and courgettes and toss together. Arrange the lettuce leaves on a platter and spoon the salad into the centre.

Serves 6.

Serving Soups. *Pasta soups are normally served from the pan into soup bowls or from a tureen placed on the table. For heavy soups containing beans, a small jug of good olive oil should be on the table. The oil both flavours the soup and cools it down.*

Fettuccine Silverbeet and Parma Ham Salad

The combination of roasted pine nuts, piquant Parmesan cheese and well-seasoned Parma ham with silverbeet and fettuccine makes an unusual Italian-style salad. You can use lasagnette, flat ribbon ruffled-edge pasta instead of fettuccine and well-rinsed tender young spinach instead of silverbeet if you prefer. Whichever way you make it it is a most delicious dish.

1 tablespoon olive oil	Salt and pepper
350 g/12 oz Parma ham (prosciutto), trimmed of fat	400 g/14 oz fettuccine
90 g/3 oz/¾ cup pine nuts, toasted (p. 36)	400 g/14 oz fettuccine
250 ml/8 fl oz/1 cup olive oil	1 bunch washed and dried silverbeet, stems
1 garlic clove	removed, leaves torn into pieces
125 ml/4 fl oz/½ cup white wine vinegar	90 g/3 oz/¾ cup Parmesan cheese, grated
1 tablespoon Dijon mustard	3 hard-boiled eggs (p. 23), chopped

Heat the oil in a frying pan and fry the Parma ham until crisp. Allow to cool and tear into pieces. Place 60 g/2 oz/½ cup of the pine nuts in a food processor or blender with the olive oil and garlic. Process until the pine nuts are well crushed. Add the vinegar, mustard, salt and pepper. Process until the dressing combines.

Cook the fettuccine (p. 14). Drain, rinse under cold water until cool and leave to stand.

Place the washed and dried silverbeet leaves in a large bowl with the dressing and leave to stand for 10 minutes. Add the fettuccine, the Parmesan cheese and most of the Parma ham. Mix together lightly. When ready to serve, arrange in a salad bowl or on a platter. Add the remaining Parma ham, Parmesan cheese and pine nuts. Sprinkle with the chopped egg and some extra pepper.

Serves 6.

Overleaf: Pesto Genovese with Ruoti (left) (p.15), Polpette Pommarola (top right) (p.31) and Pork Cannelloni Parmesan (right) (p.44) make a colourful and appetising display.

Hard-Boiled Eggs

Place the eggs in a saucepan and cover with cold water.	*Bring to the boil and cook for about 12 minutes.*	*Pour off the water and hold eggs under cold running water until cool.*	*When cold, tap shell gently to break it. Peel.*

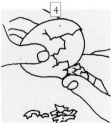

Spirale with Chicken, Chives and Thyme (top) and Fettuccine, Silverbeet and Parma Ham Salad (p. 23). Both salads make imaginative use of pasta.

Spirale with Chicken, Chives and Thyme

350 g/12 oz spirale
60 g/2 oz/¼ cup butter
Grated peel of 1 lemon
4 tablespoons lemon juice
300 ml/½ pint/1¼ cups single (light) cream

2 tablespoons snipped chives
1 tablespoon chopped thyme
450 g/1 lb/3 cups cooked chicken, chopped
60 g/2 oz/½ cup finely grated Parmesan cheese
Chives, to garnish

Cook spirale (p. 14). Drain, rinse and leave to stand. Melt the butter in a saucepan, add the lemon peel and juice. Stir to combine, then add the cream, herbs, chicken and spirale. Toss lightly together until heated through. Spoon into a bowl, sprinkle with the Parmesan cheese and garnish with chives. Serve as a warm salad with a separate bowl of tossed mixed lettuces.
Serves 4.

Pasta with Sauces

Every day someone invents new recipes and ideas for enjoying and serving pasta. With long or short pasta it is now generally accepted that anything goes.

There are two important rules, however, which you must always remember.

1. Unless the dish is a cold one, pasta must be served piping hot. Speed is essential. As soon as your pasta is cooked, it must be drained into a large warm bowl, and very quickly spooned into individual bowls or on to a platter and sauced.

2. The pasta must not be overcooked. Follow the simple instructions (p. 14) for perfectly cooked *al dente* results.

Pasta, today is often served as a single-dish meal accompanied by a tossed salad, crusty breads and a light crisp chilled white or cooled rosé wine if the pasta sauce is vegetable or meat-based. To complete the meal, serve fresh fruit and cheeses or a light tangy dessert. Pasta dishes are an excellent choice if you are cooking for a crowd. Cook two or three different kinds of pasta and give your guests a choice of sauces.

The following recipes complement the wide variety of pastas available and are easy, quick to make and delicious to eat.

Linguine Carbonara with Chicken

A welcome change from pasta and tomato sauce, carbonara is a Roman dish in which matchsticks of ham, cooked in butter, are tossed into freshly cooked hot pasta with beaten eggs and Parmesan cheese. The result is a delicious creamy-sauced pasta. Try this colourful recipe.

30 g/1 oz/2 tablespoons butter
1 red pepper (capsicum, bell pepper), thinly sliced
6 spring onions (scallions), chopped
250 g/9 oz cooked chicken breast, cut into strips

400 g/14 oz linguine or spaghetti
4 eggs, beaten
90 g/3 oz/³⁄₄ cup grated Parmesan cheese
Salt and pepper

Melt the butter in a heavy-based saucepan. Cook the pepper and spring onions over a low heat for about 5 minutes until soft.

Cook the pasta until *al dente* (p. 14). Drain thoroughly and add to the red pepper mixture. Add the chicken strips, toss together until heated through. Remove from the heat, add the eggs and half the Parmesan cheese. Season with salt and pepper. Toss until the eggs turn creamy yellow and cling to the pasta. Add the remaining Parmesan and serve immediately in warm bowls.

Serves 4-6.

Left and above: Spaghetti Puttanesca. An easy pasta dish which involves tossing all the ingredients into freshly cooked pasta. This variation introduces tuna, orange and a dash of chilli—enjoy it with a salad.

Spaghetti Puttanesca

Known as Roman whore's spaghetti, this variation adds tuna, some orange peel and juice, and a dash of chilli to the original recipe.

3 tablespoons virgin olive oil

1 red onion, thinly sliced

4 garlic cloves, crushed

6 tomatoes, peeled and seeded, coarsely chopped
(p. 30)

4 anchovy fillets, soaked in cold water for
10 minutes, dried and mashed

3 tablespoons capers, chopped

90 g/3 oz/⅔ cup black olives, stoned (pitted)
(p. 32), chopped

1 tablespoon tomato paste

400 g/14 oz spaghetti or linguine

175 g/6 oz can tuna in oil, drained

Coarsely grated peel of 1 orange

Juice of 1 orange

Red pepper (capsicum, bell pepper)
flakes/chilli flakes

3 tablespoons chopped parsley

Heat the oil in a large frying pan (skillet). Add the onions and garlic and cook for about 5 minutes or until soft.

Add the tomatoes, anchovy fillets, capers, black olives, tomato paste and orange juice. Simmer for about 10 minutes. Cook the spaghetti until *al dente* (p. 14). Drain and immediately toss into the pan, adding the tuna, orange peel, red pepper flakes to taste and parsley. Toss together, pour on to a warm platter and serve.

Serves 4-6.

Spaghetti with Garlic and Oil (Spaghetti Aglio e Olio)

A good quality, deep yellow, strong-flavoured olive oil is essential for this pasta's success. Simply tossed into cooked spaghetti with as much chopped garlic as you like, some herbs or sliced chillies as a variation, it is an easy dish to prepare. Parmesan cheese can be added, but it is not traditional.

400 g/14 oz spaghetti
Salt and pepper

125 ml/4 fl oz/½ cup olive oil
2-5 garlic cloves, finely chopped

Cook the spaghetti until *al dente* (p. 14). Drain and transfer to a warm bowl. Barely warm the olive oil and garlic in a small pan, then pour it over the pasta and toss together. Season with salt and pepper.

Serves 4.

Smoked Salmon Tagliatelle

300 ml/½ pint/1¼ cups double (heavy) cream
2 tablespoons brandy
¼ teaspoon cayenne pepper
1 small piece lemon peel
Generous pinch of grated nutmeg

400 g/14 oz tagliatelle
Salt
60 g/2 oz/¼ cup butter, cut into pieces
400 g/14 oz smoked salmon, chopped

Put the cream in a bowl with the brandy, cayenne pepper, lemon peel and nutmeg, and heat over a pan of simmering water. Cook the tagliatelle until *al dente* (p. 14). Drain and return to the saucepan. Mix in the butter and add the salmon. Remove the lemon peel from the cream and pour the sauce over the pasta. Mix together very gently, pour out on to a serving platter and serve immediately.

Serves 4.

Peeling Tomatoes

| *Cut out the core with a small knife.* | *Plunge into boiling water for 1–2 minutes.* | *Refresh under running water.* | *Skin lifts off easily with a small knife.* |

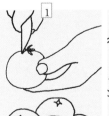

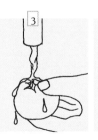
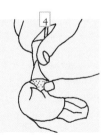

Polpette Pommarola

Polpette are meat balls. These ones are made from finely minced topside (ground) or veal and pork.

450 g/16 oz finely minced (ground) beef or veal
    and pork
1 egg
2 garlic cloves, crushed
1 onion, finely chopped
1 teaspoon oregano
3 tablespoons chopped parsley
30 g/1 oz/½ cup fresh breadcrumbs

Salt and pepper
1 quantity Fresh Tomato Sauce (p. 18) or Quick
    Tomato Sauce (p. 18)
200 g/7 oz green tagliatelle or fettuccine
200 g/7 oz yellow tagliatelle or fettuccine
Italian (flat-leaf) parsley, to garnish
Grated Parmesan cheese, to serve

Place the beef or veal and pork mince in a bowl. Add the egg, garlic, onion, oregano, parsley and breadcrumbs. Season well with salt and pepper. Mix together thoroughly. Shape into 16 polpette and leave to stand. Pour pommarola sauce into a large frying pan (skillet). Bring to the boil, add the polpette in a single layer, cover and simmer for 10 minutes or until tender, turning the polpette once with a slotted spoon during cooking, or alternatively, shaking the pan gently to prevent the polpette sticking to the base. Cook the tagliatelle until *al dente* (p. 14). Drain and transfer to a serving platter. Spoon the polpette and sauce over the pasta, garnish with parsley and serve with Parmesan cheese.
Serves 4.

Polpetti Pommarola in preparation. The meat mixture is shaped into polpetti or meatballs before the tomato sauce is cooked.

Pitting Olives

Cut across the top of the olive with a sharp knife, but not right through.	Keeping the blade on the stone, cut round the olive lengthwise.	Twist the two sides against each other to separate.	Using the tip of the knife, release the stone gently.

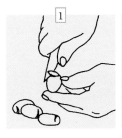 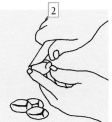 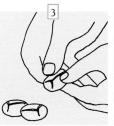 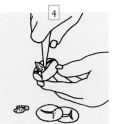

Tagliarini with Tapenade

Any quick-cooking pasta of similar size to tagliarini is ideal for this recipe. The blended olive oil sauce is cold, like a pesto, and the whole dish makes a tasty light meal. It is a most colourful dish with black and green olives and sun-dried tomatoes.

15 black olives, stoned (pitted) (p. 32)
15 stuffed green olives
2 garlic cloves
4 tablespoons olive oil
1 tablespoon fresh white breadcrumbs

Salt and pepper
1 teaspoon lemon juice
400 g/14 oz tagliarini
3 tablespoons chopped parsley, to garnish
8 sun-dried tomatoes, cut into fine strips

Place the black and green olives in a food processor or blender with the garlic. Process, pouring in the oil to make a fairly smooth paste. Add the breadcrumbs, season with salt and pepper and add the lemon juice. Process for 1–2 seconds to combine. Cook the tagliarini or other pasta until *al dente* (p. 14). Drain and return to the saucepan. Add the olive sauce and toss together well. Add a little more oil if the pasta is too dry. Transfer to a warm serving platter, sprinkle with parsley and sun-dried tomato strips.
Serves 4.

Penne Peperoni with Walnuts

Red, green or yellow peppers (capsicums, bell peppers) add a sweetish flavour to a quick tomato sauce with its dash of curry powder. Any tubular short pasta is suitable and the walnuts must be as fresh as you can buy.

250 g/9 oz penne
400 g/14 oz can peeled tomatoes
1 large garlic clove, peeled
3 teaspoons curry powder
4 tablespoons tomato paste
125 ml/4 fl oz/½ cup water
2 tablespoons olive oil

125 g/4 oz/1 cup shelled walnuts
1 large red pepper (capsicum, bell pepper), cut into
    strips or squares
1 large green pepper (capsicum, bell pepper), cut
    into strips or squares
Italian (flat-leaf) parsley leaves, to garnish

Cook the penne until *al dente* (p. 14). Drain and leave to stand.

Place the tomatoes, garlic, curry powder and tomato paste in a food processor or blender. Process until smooth. Pour into a saucepan, add the water, cover and simmer for 15 minutes. Heat the oil in a saucepan, sauté the walnuts until golden, remove and drain on a paper towel. Add the peppers to the pan, and cook over a low heat until just tender. Return the penne to the pan, toss until the mixture is heated through.

Spoon the tomato sauce on to plates or into bowls. Top with the pasta mixture, scatter the walnuts and parsley over the mixture. Alternatively spoon the sauce over the pasta mixture and serve.

Serves 4.

Conchiglie Marinara

This is an unusual combination of shell pasta and a seafood tomato sauce with mushrooms and hot chilli. Although you can choose whatever seafood you prefer, squid is important in the mix. It could be used on its own as a variation.

6 tablespoons olive oil
1 small onion, diced
1 small carrot, diced
225 g/8 oz assorted cleaned squid
125 ml/4 fl oz/½ cup dry white wine
400 g/14 oz can peeled tomatoes or fresh tomatoes,
    peeled and puréed (p. 30)

½ chilli, chopped
Salt and pepper
400 g/14 oz conchiglie or other short pasta
225 g/8 oz/3 cups shelled prawns, (shrimp) and scallops
125 g/4 oz/1½ cups button mushrooms, thinly sliced
    or other firm white fish, cut into dice
3 tablespoons chopped parsley

Heat the oil in a saucepan, add the onion, carrot and squid, cook over a low heat for about 5 minutes. Increase the heat to high, add the wine and cook until it evaporates. Add the tomatoes, chilli, salt and pepper. Simmer for 30 minutes or until the squid is tender.

Meanwhile cook the conchiglie until *al dente* (p. 14). Drain, transfer to a warm bowl, cover and leave to stand. Add the remaining choice of seafood and mushrooms to the sauce, simmer for a further 8–10 minutes.

Pour the sauce over the pasta, adding the parsley and serve.

Serves 4.

Above: Ricotta and Nut Pasta. The pine nuts or almonds are cooked in butter until lightly browned, then the pasta, ricotta and other ingredients are tossed in to make this quick pasta.
Right: A delicious light dish, using any short pasta. Cooked to al dente perfection.

Ricotta and Nut Pasta

Almost any of the shorter pastas such as elbow macaroni, penne, fusilli, farfalle or conchiglie are ideal in this quick dish. Once cooked they combine perfectly with fresh ricotta cheese. It will probably become one of your favourite dishes.

375 g/13 oz any short pasta	250 g/9 oz/generous 1 cup ricotta cheese, mashed
60 g/2 oz/¼ cup butter	5 tablespoons chopped parsley
60 g/2 oz/½ cup pine nuts or flaked (slivered) almonds	½ teaspoon grated nutmeg
125 g/4 oz sliced mortadella or salami, cut into strips	Pepper

Cook pasta until *al dente* (p. 14). Drain and transfer back to the saucepan. Leave to stand. Melt the butter in a pan, add the nuts and cook until lightly browned. Add the nuts to the pasta with the remaining ingredients. Toss together with two spoons and cook over a low heat until heated through. Season with pepper and serve immediately.
Serves 4.

Ways of Reheating Pasta

(a) Place the pasta in a heatproof bowl and add enough boiling water to cover it. Leave it to stand for 1 minute, then drain well.

(b) Alternatively, place the pasta in a large sieve (strainer) and plunge into a saucepan of boiling water for a few seconds. Remove, shake gently to drain and remove excess water.

(c) If you have a microwave oven, place the pasta in a microwave-safe bowl with 250 ml/8 fl oz/1 cup hot water. Cover, microwave on High for 1 minute. Remove, stir and continue heating, checking at 1 minute intervals, until heated through.

Macaroni with Ham and Peas

This light, delicious pasta can be made from ingredients already on hand. You can use any cooked sliced Italian-style sausage as an alternative to the ham.

2 tablespoons olive oil	150 g/5 oz thickly cut cooked ham, cut into strips
60 g/2 oz/¼ cup (or ½ stick) butter	Salt and pepper
1 small onion, finely chopped	400 g/14 oz elbow macaroni or penne
300 g/11 oz/¾ cup shelled fresh or frozen peas	60 g/2 oz/½ cup Gruyère cheese, cubed
6 tablespoons chicken stock	60 g/2 oz/½ cup Parmesan cheese, grated

Heat the oil and half the butter in a frying pan (skillet), add the onion and cook over a low heat until softened. Add the peas, continue to cook, adding a little of the stock occasionally to prevent the mixture drying out. In a separate pan melt the remaining butter, fry the ham until slightly crisp and then add it to the pea mixture. Season with salt and pepper and keep warm until required. Cook the pasta until *al dente* (p. 14), drain and transfer to a warm bowl. Pour the pea and ham mixture over it and toss together, adding the cheeses as you mix so that they melt as much as possible. Serve immediately.
Serves 4.

To Toast Nuts (pine nuts)

In oven. Spread the nuts on a baking sheet. Bake in a preheated oven at 180°C/350°F/Gas 4 for about 4 minutes. Remove from the oven, shake the baking sheet or turn nuts over. Bake for a further couple of minutes or until golden. Remove immediately from the hot baking sheet, to stop the nuts from cooking further. Avoid using black baking sheets as they get hot too quickly..

Dry-frying. Dry-fry by placing the nuts in a pan over a low-to-moderate heat for 2-4 minutes, shaking the pan to turn nuts so that they colour evenly.

Rigatoni with Broccoli. The robust vegetable sauce simmers in a pan for only 15 minutes.

Rigatoni with Broccoli

The islands of Italy follow the southern style of cooking and this dish is no exception. Raisins, pine nuts, pecorino cheese and anchovies add a Sicilian flavour. Rigatoni is an excellent base for this dish, but you can use whatever short pasta you have in your store cupboard.

350 g/12 oz broccoli, cut into florets
3 tablespoons olive oil
1 onion, sliced
400 g/14 oz peeled ripe tomatoes (p. 30),
   chopped
Pepper
350 g/12 oz Rigatoni or other pasta

1 garlic clove, chopped
6 anchovies, drained (p. 38)
5 tablespoons seedless raisins, soaked in warm
   water for about 15 minutes
5 tablespoons pine nuts
4 large basil leaves, torn into pieces
90 g/3 oz/¾ cup grated pecorino cheese, to serve

Preparing Anchovies

Drain the anchovies of oil in a small sieve.   Soak them in milk or water for a few minutes.   Drain again.   Split each anchovy in half, lengthwise.

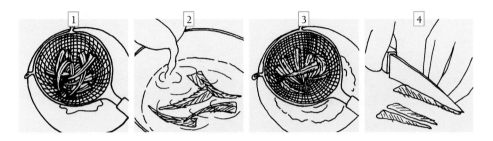

Cook the broccoli in boiling salted water for 5–10 minutes until tender. Drain thoroughly and leave to stand. Heat half the oil in a frying pan (skillet), add the onion and cook over a low heat for 5 minutes. Add the tomatoes, season with pepper, cover and simmer for 10 minutes.

Meanwhile cook the pasta until *al dente* (p. 14). Drain, and transfer to a warm bowl.

Heat the remaining oil in another small pan, add the garlic and cook gently until browned. Add the anchovies and cook for a further minute. Add the mixture to the tomato sauce with the raisins, broccoli and pine nuts. Cook for a further 5 minutes, stirring frequently. Pour the sauce over the rigatoni, add the basil leaves, fold gently to combine and serve immediately with pecorino cheese.

Serves 4.

Ways of Serving Pasta

(a) Place the pasta with the sauce in a heated serving bowl from which it is easy to extract the pasta. Pour the sauce over the top. Using two forks, toss until the pasta is well coated. Serve by passing the bowl around the table for people to help themselves. Accompany the dish with grated Parmesan cheese.

(b) Place the pasta in a heated bowl, transfer it to a flat platter, pour on a little sauce and sprinkle with cheese.

(c) Place the pasta in a heated serving bowl or on a platter with a minimum of sauce and put the rest of the sauce in a bowl on the table. People can then add as much sauce as they want.

(d) Cook and drain the pasta and arrange in individual warm bowls topped with sauce and cheese.

In Italy all forms of pasta are eaten from a soup plate.

Rigatoni with Broccoli. Crusty bread and Pecorino cheese accompany this Sicilian-style pasta.

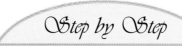

Step by Step

Pasta with Fillings

In the vast repertoire of Italian cooking, every region has its speciality, yet the principle of filling pasta is the same—delicious stuffings encased in a fine shell of fresh pasta which is cooked until *al dente*, or simmered in a broth, or layered with meat, chicken or fish sauces, béchamel or vegetable–cheese mixtures and baked to perfection. If you have time or it is a special occasion make your own pasta for ravioli (p. 12) and use the homemade pasta to create lasagne, by cutting the rolled dough into sheets about 20 x 15 cm/8 x 6 inches. Speciality shops, delicatessens and supermarkets, however, supply the pastas that are the starting point for these dishes. All you need to do is make the sauces.

Nothing can surpass a bowl of tender ravioli coated in a basil butter and Parmesan; cannelloni tubes filled with ricotta and spinach; or popular seasoned minced (ground) meats or lasagne sheets uniquely presented as a base for a simmered, sauced cacciatore-style chicken and black olive casserole.

Left: Parmesan Ricotta Ravioli. Immediately they are cooked, serve with Tomato (p. 18) or Bolognaise Sauce (p. 17)and freshly grated Parmesan cheese. Below: Cut the prepared dough into 4 pieces and as you roll each piece, keep the others covered to prevent them drying out.

Parmesan Ricotta Ravioli

It is fun to stuff your own pasta. This ravioli recipe is easy and you can vary the filling by adding to the ricotta, spinach that has been pressed in a sieve (or strainer) or squeezed to remove all the moisture to the ricotta. Complement the ravioli with any of the Classic Sauces (p. 15). For an even simpler dish, top with melted butter, lots of Parmesan cheese and a sprinkling of pepper.

225 g/8 oz/2 cups plain (all-purpose) flour
2 eggs
2 egg whites
6 teaspoons olive oil
2 teaspoons salt
Water

RICOTTA FILLING
250 g/9 oz/generous 1 cup ricotta cheese
60 g/2 oz/½ cup grated Parmesan cheese
1 egg
½ teaspoon nutmeg
Salt and pepper to taste

To make the pasta, place the flour into a large bowl, make a well in the centre and add the remaining ingredients. Mix together with a fork until the dough can be gathered into a rough ball, adding a little water if dough is too dry. Knead the dough for about 10 minutes on a floured board, until smooth, shiny and elastic, working in extra flour if the dough seems sticky. Wrap in clingfilm (plastic wrap) and leave to stand for 10 minutes before rolling. Mix the filling ingredients together in a bowl.

Divide the pasta dough into four pieces and roll out the first piece as thinly as possible to about a 30 cm/12 inch square. Cover the rolled pasta with a damp tea-towel (dish cloth) to prevent it drying and then roll out the second piece of dough to a similar size and shape. Using the first sheet of rolled out pasta as a sort of chessboard, place a small teaspoonful of the ricotta mixture every 5 cm/2 inches across and down the pasta dough.

Dip a pastry brush or finger into a bowl of water and make even vertical and horizontal lines in a chessboard pattern on the sheet of pasta between the spoonfuls of cheese mixture. Carefully

Making Ravioli

Roll out fresh pasta. Place a teaspoon of ricotta mixture every 5 cm/2 inches.	*With a wet finger, make vertical and horizontal lines on the pasta.*	*Place another sheet of pasta on top. Press on to wet lines around filling.*	*Using a small knife, cut the pasta into squares along the wet lines.*

To make a Stuffed Pasta Salad. *Cook 350 g/12 oz tortellini or ravioli until tender, drain and allow to cool. Combine with some rinsed curly endive (chicory), mignonette lettuce leaves and 250 g/9 oz cherry tomatoes together in a bowl. Combine about 125 ml/4 fl oz/½ cup olive oil, 2 tablespoons balsamic vinegar, 2 teaspoons lemon juice, 1 crushed garlic clove and 2 teaspoons torn basil leaves in a bowl. Whisk together and pour it over the salad.*

place the second sheet of rolled out pasta on top of the first one, pressing down firmly around the filling and along the wetted lines. Cut the pasta into squares along the wetted lines using a ravioli cutter, a pastry wheel or a small sharp knife. Separate the mounds of ravioli and place them on greaseproof (waxed) paper. Roll out, fill and cut the two other portions of dough. Set aside until required.

To cook, drop the ravioli into about 5 litres/9 pints/5½ quarts of rapidly boiling, salted water and stir them gently with a wooden spoon to prevent them from sticking to one another or to the bottom of the pan. Boil for about 10 minutes or until they are tender and rise to the surface. Drain the ravioli in a large sieve (strainer) or colander (perforated strainer). Serve immediately with either Fresh Tomato Sauce (p. 18) or Bolognese Sauce (p. 17).

Makes about 50 ravioli and serves 6-8.

Variation

Omit Parmesan cheese. Thaw a 250 g/9 oz packet of frozen spinach, squeeze it well or pressed it in a sieve (strainer) to remove all moisture. Stir it into the ricotta cheese, egg and nutmeg mixture. Season with salt and pepper.

Parmesan Ricotta Ravioli. Teaspoonful of ricotta mixture at 5 cm/2 inch intervals across and down the rolled-out dough create a chess or chequerboard effect.

Ravioli with Avocado Cream

Buy your ravioli with a spinach and ricotta filling or have a supply in your freezer for this quick pasta dish. The avocado cream requires no cooking and adds a subtle flavour.

1 ripe avocado
150 ml/¼ pint/⅔ cup single (light) cream

125 g/4 oz/1 cup grated Parmesan cheese
24–32 fresh dried ravioli

Scoop out the flesh from the avocado (below) and place it in a bowl with the cream. Mash with a fork or process in a food processor or blender until smooth. Season lightly with salt and pepper. Mix in the Parmesan cheese.

Cook the ravioli (p. 14). If using dried ravioli you will need to cook it a little longer than the fresh. Serve immediately in bowls, allowing 6-8 ravioli per person. Spoon the avocado cream over the ravioli and serve with extra grated Parmesan cheese.
Serves 4.

Stoning (Pitting) an Avocado. *Be sure the avocado is ripe (yielding when pressed lightly at the edge). Cut in half lengthwise and twist to separate halves. Hold the half with the stone in your hand, and gently squeeze. This may release the stone. If not, with a sharp chopping knife, make a quick cut into the stone and lift. The stone will come out on the knife.*

Pork Cannelloni Parmesan

Lasagne sheets make an easy alternative to filling cannelloni tubes. Instead of using the pork filling, you can substitute ricotta cheese mixed with chopped ham, spinach, basil and tomatoes, or Parmesan cheese and pine nuts. You can vary the sauce too. Try the Quick Tomato Sauce (p. 18).

1 tablespoon butter
1 large onion, chopped
1 carrot, chopped
1 celery stick, chopped
500 g/18 oz/4½ cups lean minced (ground) pork
2 tablespoons Marsala wine
30 g/1 oz button mushrooms, chopped

3 tablespoons tomato paste
Salt and pepper
300 g/11 oz/8 sheets (about 20 x 15 cm/8 x 6 inches)
  fresh lasagne
250 ml/8 fl oz/1 cup béchamel sauce (p. 16)
60 g/2 oz/½ cup grated Parmesan cheese

Melt the butter in a pan. Add the onion, carrot, celery and pork. Simmer for 10 minutes, stirring regularly, then add the Marsala. Allow the fumes to evaporate, then add the mushrooms and tomato paste. Season with salt and pepper and continue to simmer for 30 minutes. Dilute with a little boiling water if the mixture appears too thick.

Meanwhile cook the lasagne sheets, four at a time, in plenty of boiling salted water. Lift out and drain them side by side on wet cloths to prevent them from sticking together. Put 2 tablespoonfuls of the filling on each sheet of lasagna, roll up and put them in a single layer, in a buttered shallow ovenproof dish. Cover with the béchamel sauce and sprinkle with the Parmesan cheese. Bake in a preheated oven at 200°C/400°F/gas 6 for 20 minutes or until the cheese is golden brown and the sauce is bubbling hot. Remove and leave to stand for 5 minutes.
Serves 4 as a main dish or 8 as an entrée.

Chicken Niçoise with Lasagne

This dish, a wonderful pan-simmered casserole rich in tomato flavour, is a variation of chicken cacciatore or huntsman's chicken. You can use lasagne verdi (green) or pappardelle pasta for variety.

5 tablespoons olive oil
1.5 kg/3 lb chicken, cut into 8 pieces
1 onion, chopped
2 garlic cloves, chopped
125 g/4 oz/⅔ cup rashers (slices) bacon, rind removed, roughly chopped
125 ml/4 fl oz/½ cup dry white or red wine

1 kg/2½ lb fresh ripe tomatoes, chopped or 2 x 400 g/14 oz cans peeled tomatoes
4 tablespoons tomato paste
Salt and pepper
400 g/14 oz fresh or dried, plain or green lasagne sheets
12 black olives, to garnish
Grated Parmesan cheese, to serve

Heat the oil in a pan (skillet). Add the chicken pieces and sauté carefully, turning them until they are lightly browned. Put on a paper towel and leave to drain. Add the onion, garlic and bacon, and cook until the onion softens. Add the wine and allow to evaporate. Put the chicken back in the pan, and add the fresh or canned tomatoes and purée. Season with salt and pepper, stir to combine, cover and simmer for about 30 minutes, stirring occasionally.

Cut the lasagne sheets in half or into smaller portions if necessary. Cook until *al dente* (p. 14), drain, and transfer to a shallow bowl. Pour half the sauce over the pasta and toss lightly.

Arrange the chicken on top, spoon the remaining sauce over the pieces, garnish with the olives and serve with the Parmesan cheese.
Serves 4.

Lasagne Bolognese. *Use 400 g/14 oz/12 sheets cooked lasagne, 1 quantity each of Bolognese sauce and Béchamel sauce (p. 16) and about 175 g/6 oz/1½ cups grated mozzarella or Parmesan cheese. Assemble and bake the lasagne (p. 46).*

Spinach Lasagne

Known all over the world, there are many different styles of lasagne. Traditionally, cooked flat sheets of pasta are layered with a béchamel sauce, tomato or meat sauce topped with mozzarella and Parmesan cheese and oven-baked. Here is a delicious version using layers of spinach, ricotta and Parmesan cheeses, with a veal, mushroom and bacon sauce and fresh lasagne. If you can't buy fresh lasagne, use 12 dried lasagne sheets and cook for about 8-10 minutes until al dente.

400 g/14 oz/12 sheets (about 20 x 15 cm/8 x 6
   inches) fresh lasagne
4 tablespoons olive oil
75 g/2½ oz/½ cup bacon, chopped
1 onion, chopped
250 g/9 oz minced (ground) veal
60 g/2 oz/⅓ cup chicken livers, finely chopped
60 g/2 oz/¾ cup button mushrooms, chopped
4 tablespoons tomato paste, diluted in
   4 tablespoons boiling water

Salt and pepper
675 g/1½ lb cooked spinach
250 g/9 oz/generous 1 cup Ricotta cheese
2 tablespoons double (heavy) cream
125 g/4 oz/1 cup Parmesan cheese, grated
1 egg
Grated nutmeg
60 g/2 oz/¼ cup butter for greasing

Cook the lasagne, four at a time, for about 3 minutes. Lift out with a large slotted spoon and lay them carefully on a wet cloth, side by side, to drain.

Heat the oil in a saucepan, sauté the bacon and onion until the onion softens. Add the veal and brown it lightly, stirring continuously. Add the chicken livers and mushrooms. Mix together thoroughly. Pour in the diluted tomato paste and season with salt and pepper. Cover and simmer for about 20 minutes, stirring occasionally. Add a little extra boiling water if the mixture appears to be drying out.

Chop the spinach finely, place in a bowl with the ricotta cheese. Add the cream, half the Parmesan, and the egg. Season with nutmeg, salt and pepper. Beat thoroughly until combined. Use half the butter to grease a large ovenproof dish (about 30 x 20 cm/12 x 8 inches) generously. Place a layer of lasagne on the bottom and cover with a layer of the veal sauce. Add another layer of lasagne and spread a layer of the spinach mixture over it. Continue alternating the veal and spinach mixtures with the lasagne sheets, ending with the meat sauce. Sprinkle with the remaining Parmesan cheese and dot the remaining butter on top. Place in a preheated oven at 200°C/400°F/gas 6 and bake for about 20 minutes or until bubbling and golden brown. Remove and leave to stand for about 5 minutes before cutting into squares.
Serves 6.

Serving Baked Pastas. *Place baked pastas in their ovenproof dish on a flat serving platter with a folded napkin on it. No cheese is normally offered at the table with baked pasta dishes.*

Spinach Lasagne. Layers of cooked lasagne being placed in the baking dish with the meat sauce.

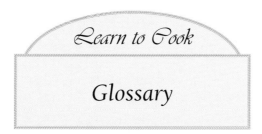

Learn to Cook

Glossary

Al dente Meaning literally 'to the bite' this term is applied to the degree a pasta is cooked. It should have no hard white uncooked central core, but should also not be overcooked and soggy.

Anchovies Very strong tasting, small salty filleted fish, often bottled in oil or brine.

Bacon Purchased in slices or in a piece to be cut as required. It is also known as pancetta in Italian cuisine.

Balsamic vinegar A vinegar aged in wooden casks with a sweet, sharp flavour. It is commonly used on salads and in some sauces.

Boil To cook in water or a liquid until bubbles rise continually and break on the surface.

Capers Pickled buds of a Mediterranean shrub.

Dice To cut into small, even cubes.

Florets Small, uniform pieces of broccoli or cauliflower prepared with very little stalk.

Gruyère A Swiss cheese with small holes and a nutty, slightly salty flavour.

Knead To manipulate a dough with a pressing, folding and stretching motion to make the dough pliable and smooth.

Mortadella A large pink roll of preserved meat. The term also refers to pressed pork meat that has large white spots and sometimes contains pieces of pistachio nut.

Olive oil This comes in several different grades, each grade having a different flavour. The most flavoursome is the extra virgin variety, which is the purest quality virgin oil, obtained from the pulp of high-grade fruit. Pure olive oil is pressed from the pulp and kernels of second-grade olives. Extra light olive oil is lighter in colour and flavour than pure and virgin.

Parmesan cheese A golden, crumbly, hard-grating and slightly salty-tasting cheese eaten with and on pasta. The older the cheese, the harder and stronger tasting it will be. It is made from cow's milk and has a high protein and fat content.

Pecorino This is very similar to Parmesan cheese, but is made from ewe's milk and is often seen in shops studded with peppercorns.

Pine nuts Small, oval-shaped, creamy-coloured kernels.

Prosciutto (Parma ham): Uncooked, unsmoked, cured delicate-tasting ham.

Purée To press through a sieve or to process in a food processor to produce a smooth thick mixture.

Ricotta cheese A mildly flavoured, soft, white cheese commonly used in fillings for stuffed and baked pasta. It is also used in sweet dishes.

Roux Melted butter and flour which is cooked over a low heat to which milk, stock or wine is added. This is the base for many sauces and soups.

Saffron Stamens from a crocus plant. It imparts a bright yellow colour to food.

Salami Usually made of finely minced (ground) pure pork or a mixture of pork and beef, mildly or highly spiced, coarse or fine textured. They are available in many shapes and sizes.

Sauté To cook in oil or butter in a pan (skillet) over low heat.

Sun-dried tomatoes Dried tomatoes commonly bottled in oil. They have a concentrated flavour.

Sieve To pass through a sieve in order to reduce to a pulp or remove lumps.

Simmer To cook in liquid over a very low heat so that the liquid barely bubbles.

Tomato paste This concentrated, pure and natural tomato purée is made by evaporating all moisture from fresh tomatoes.